Love Letters

to Sophie's Mom

By Rob Bignell

Atiswinic Press · Ojai, Calif.

GW00670545

LOVE LETTERS TO SOPHIE'S MOM

Copyright Rob Bignell, 2012

Atiswinic Press
Ojai, Calif. 93023
http://inventingreality.4t.com/
loveletterstosophiesmom.html

ISBN 978-0-9858739-1-2

Manufactured in the United States of America
First printing September 2012

DEDICATION

"I love you without knowing how, or when, or from where.
"I love you straightforwardly, without complexities or pride;
"So I love you because I know no other way."

- Pablo Neruda, "Sonnet XVII"

For J.A.R.

ACKNOWLEDGEMENTS

Thank you to Mary, Stephanie, Mark and Judith for your insightful and invaluable critiques of these writings.

Contents

The Dance

They stir coffee at first, just a little honey and milk,
Sit across from one another, an aroma rich and alluring
Rising between. "Hey, long time, no talk," she says.
He fingers his mug, eyes hers at the table's other end,
Says, "I'd forgotten how sweet your voice was." Her mouth
    curves adoringly,
She leans back slightly, brings red mug to dewy
Lips, yet her long gaze stays on him. "But not your smile," he
    adds.
They sip once more; their set mugs shift closer. They recall
    people, places
They both once knew but that now seem no more real
Than the white clouds in their coffee. "Time is a thief," he
    says.
"The family, the kids." "The growing old together, the
    career."
"The lemonade on the front porch rocking chairs."
They pause, awhirl in one another's dreams. "The talking
    hours
On end." His head bows, the mug dips with it as if in
    aerobatic
Display; he looks up. "Are we going to be
Alone the rest of our lives?" Steam rises from their mugs,
    now side by side;
Their voices fall softer so only the other hears. She pushes
    her
Hair back behind an ear. Their coffee mugs sit
Askance, circling one another; her mug's handle points
In a different direction than before, as if pirouetting.
"We are supposed to do something with these

Damn hearts of ours, and we are meant to love and be
   loved."
They both know the truth. They smile at one another, they
   drink once again,
Each mug palmed in their hands warm as a heart.

Portrait of You as a Young Girl

I see you hunting for white violets in springtime
As a golden-face child skipping, skitter stepping
Through grass meadows and woods, chattering of life near
A flowing brook. Your laughter is musical chimes
Keeping perfect rhythm to the wind sweeping through
Your hair, playfully twirling it, as eyes sparkle
In a sprinting smile. Snowy blossoms clustered
In your hand dance ringlets around your lacy sway,
Your sweet youthful breath tickling life's bountifulness.

Wherever I Walk

Wherever I walk, you are there: the round bales
On the hillside, like some painting of a French
Provencal scene, speaks of your serenity;
The doe leaping from the roadside wheat into
The thicket, of your graceful steps; white daisies
Brightening the green as if your cheerful eyes;
The curved cut into layers of granite
Statuesque like your sovereign face; tall and
Straight pines standing long-legged like you; rustle
Of leaves in the quick wind ringing as your laugh;
The orange butterfly perching on a clover
Blossom sings of your vibrancy; white baby's
Breath reminding me of the hundred lovely
Tiny things you do for me each day. My love,
It's decided: I must walk again – at once.

As Rain Mists Outside

As rain mists outside, you drift through airy
Time into a nether world of slumber
Leaving me alone to read Neruda,
Whose words float into silent nothingness.
Do deaf ears still capture those sweet patterns
Of sound that you longed to listen for
In delicate drowsiness? Do your dreams
Turn away into a cave of nightmares
Or do my rhythmic spirits shine like
Spring's sun in a land of hope and new life?
Does the fog outside now turn to violent
Storm, or does my imagery soothe sleep?
I dare pray my songs in rest sound like waves
Gently lapping against sun-drenched shores.

Enchantress

Like the night sky lit in brilliant points,
Or rippled sand of a wind-strewn desert,
The blue endlessness of ocean waters
Wide as that transparent dome above us,
Like the moving lamp bringing day and dark,
I am enchanted by you – a magic
Spell cast by a woman with power to
Whirl stars about us as if they're dancing,
Make hardest rock fruitful with verdant life,
Quicken time across great, vast horizons,
Bring heaven wherever we walk below,
Brighten midnight as if it were noontide.

Even at Night Your Glory Shines on Me

Even at night your glory shines on me
Through the reflections of the glowing moon
Catching your light, casting it back to earth,
Always there when I awake to darkness.

When nightmares stir lurking shadows in me,
Sweat bleeds, my eyes flash up toward the sky,
Then silver rays cradle me in comfort
For I feel you there, hidden yet present.

But sometimes the moon grows weary and wanes,
Abandoning me as I scan grim skies,
Desperately searching for that hint of light,
Then I calm, gaze over the horizon,

And my eyes close, for I can rest secure,
My love, knowing you will arrive like dawn.

Almuerzo in Ventura

Seated on the deck, the rhythmic waves beating
Against the shore in time with our hearts,
The whole sparkling ocean spreading infinitely
Into the horizon like our future.
Sun blazing over us like a spell, gulls
Riding air currents surrendering themselves to fate,
I tell you of the eternal surf and its salty mist.

Enchanting scent of lemon upon our plates.
We sharing, savoring bites of one
Another's pescado, filling a deep hunger.
With a smile light as water, you say, "Tell
Me once more about the eternal surf."
Your prevailing face bright as a magnolia bloom.
The marine wind tousles your hair. Our hearts sing the same
        song.

Flowers of Ojai

We walk through the park arm in arm, as if down
A center aisle, bouquets to both sides of us.
That gold daffodil stands all tall, chivalrous,
Like you, she says. And that white camellia,
Shaped like a Southern Belle dress, looks full of
Graciousness, like you, I respond. We hold one
Another, kissing before the red and white
Roses that cherish us in their unity
And purity. We amble on, hand in hand,
The myriad of blooms fragrant as your smile.
The bachelor buttons' Catalina blue
Petals reach forward in anticipation,
Linen white holly sits happy in fertile
Green nest, as cautious lavender blossoms peak
Distrustfully above their thin stems. I wrap
My arm about your trim waist as the flowers
Wave like a hymnal. Crimson azaleas
Grow with abundance upon their petite bush;
The amber marigold stands meekly nearby
Desiring to be wealthier, showier.
The pallid pink peonies appear to be
Late in bloom, as the yarrow glows with good health.
Your shadow dances over the whispering
Blossoms. If it were allowed, my young love,
I would string them into a floral headpiece
And ask for your hand until death do us part.

Hair

Raven hair tumbles down your back in waves;
I run my hand through it like an ancient
Priest wading into the holiest sea,
As if the ship captain returned home.

It falls through my fingers in graceful streams;
My hands are furrows seeking nourishment,
They cup it, but liquid soft threads spill out.
That's to be expected from a wild heart
Such as yours, I suppose, but it is what
I love most about you: that you cannot
Be bridled any more than can the wind.

My hand slips through your black ocean once more,
Draws it near so I may breathe in its scent
Of honey and olive oil as we gaze
Face to face into both our dusky eyes.

The shoreline of your temple hovers close;
You blow an untamed wisp behind your ear.
My hand tumbles through your long rivulets;
Those deep tresses run like a fast current,
Pulling my palm along until it is
Surrounded by nothing but fluid waves.
I could set sail upon it for new lands.

Gracious Sun

You lay in azure moonlight, your curves like
The gentle roll of nighttime hills, when your
Eyes turn to mine. A wet bead sparkles upon
Your skin, as if a treasure of sapphires
Brought into the sun by miners.

I caress your soft skin, it warm unlike
Any blackened horizon, then rest
My head upon your shoulders. My cheek has
Found its patch of grass, its place so my frame
Might rest.

Ever so delicately, your back rises
And falls. Your heart makes itself heard.

Slowly, faintly, the blue gossamer of
Your shape lightens until powder, until Alice,
Until white. Yet only moon shines through our
Open window. Your form brightens until
Cream, until maize, until sun glow,

As if dawn spread its wings upon you. Yet
Only dark surrounds us. Dark like the cold
Of space enveloping a star. My mind
Reels, seeking a horizon to steady
Itself.

What are hills or sky? I hold you tighter,
A world, a man, seeking your heat.

Evening in Anaheim

Violet lilacs strewn across verdant lawn,
Plucked flower floats in a deep warm pool,
Fantasies of night fill the air; the mood
Winding around high wire suspended orbs,
Cheerful laughter bounces between tables,
Wicker chairs, umbrellas blocking the stars,
Small sparkles, accepting couples' wishes,
Man, woman gaze in moonglow, now quiet,
Each lounging, kissing, parting holding hands,
Soft shoulders held tight in strong arms, comfort
For both, flight from dark loneliness to warmth,
When dawn arrives, circled in loving arms.

If I Won a Lottery

If I won a lottery, I'd spend my days writing poetry about
   you.
I'd write of how your hair twists in the wind like twirling
   leaves on an autumn gust,
Of your flesh's pearly tone, of how your eyes turning to me
   glint like the flash
Of a gold coin, of your smile that always has been the balm
   for my aching heart,
Of how your scent wafts like a gentle breeze of sun-kissed
   wildflowers, of how
Your waist curves like a silver river, of the heat of your lips
   pressed against
The nape of my neck, of how I sigh when your head settles
   against the pillow
That is my chest and my hands softly pull your hair, the
   color of darkest plum,
Back behind an ear so I may watch you slowly breathe in
   and out as you sleep,
Of how I wake to see the morning sun grace the face of the
   woman I love.
But alas, with pleasure I must admit my honey-breathed
   one, that I never
Play any lottery, for I already am the richest man in the
   world.

I'd Scatter Your Petals All over Me

The scent of roses – their fragrance reminds
Me of you, the feeling one gets drinking
Sweet wine on a day of warm spring breezes,
Blushing dizzily with romantic faith.

But these claret petals lay scattered,
Strewn across cruel spring's cold, muddied ground,
Flattened hearts. My fingers glide over
One fallen drop, it tender like your lips.

Tears running, I gather each lost petal,
This ignominious end to beauty.
Were you the season's last rose, left to bloom
Alone, I'd scatter your petals all over me.

Your Love is a Thunderstorm

Through the day, your moist heat builds. You close
Upon me until I see only
Folds of your Tyrian purple dress.
Then stillness. Your long fingers caress
My temples, shoot brilliant flashes
Of light before me. Your hot breath fills
My ear, thrumming loud as thunder.
Your lips stream across my cheek and mouth
Like a rush of rain from the heavens.
My frame trembles as if leaves under
The weight of those drops. Then gray rises
As your lips leave and you swirl away,
And I wish for your sweet storm again.

The Graces of Daybreak

I like to wake before you, to savor the graces of daybreak:

The gentle billow of the curtain in the warming breeze like the rise and fall of your bosom...

Apricot sunlight angling up the walls then down the bed, as if sheets drawing back so you may lift your lithe body from sleep...

A warbler's soft trill on the magnolia branches outside our window, sweet as your first smile...

The grass' moistness, glittering like your eyes as they first flutter open.

I am a cat burglar stealing his last jewels for the night.

Orange Peelings

You cross your bare legs, radiant in sunset's gaze,
Your eyes half closed, as if your handiwork requires
Nirvanic meditation. Gently, precisely,
You insert the knife at the orange's top, peeling
Away in circles. "Peeling an orange is meant to
Be done...elegantly," you say, your voice slipping
Across the room with our fruit's citrus scent.
A peeling drifts to the floor. Your fingers pull two
Wedges apart. Juice sprays out. You offer me one
Slice, press it against my tongue. A trickle of juice
Spreads across my lips. You kiss it off, unbutton
My shirt, peeling it away with sharp fingernail,
And rub the other sweet slice against my bare chest.

Dress

When you walk into the room, it's as if a thousand
   butterflies abruptly have taken flight.
You pirouette, showing off your new dress, hem whirling:
Spots of fiery sapphire and vermillion red, a spiritual
   vibration, as if poured onto a black veil;
Soak stains of intense, contrasting colors, watercolor-like
   and translucent, like your eyes;
Folds of gauzy cloth swirling like your laughter, virga upon
   the canvas of your body.
I see not a covering but your soul.

Lips

Your lips leave me drunk. Thin as a flute glass,
They billow like a blossoming flower
When you speak, from your lips flow the sweetest
Spirit; I must pull you close, so I feel
Your breath upon my face. I close my eyes
To brimming lips, moist as dew, satin soft,
They taste like champagne, as if my mouth just
Pulled a smooth grape from the vine. My words
Stumble. I must imbibe of them once more.

Scar

In your nakedness, is there any doubt that the angels
Tailored you? My hand gliding across your body sounds
Like the whisper of cloth shifting aside; a thread stretching
Between our tongues reflects moonlight as our lips part. My
    mouth
Works across your collarbone, around your breasts, the
    fabric
Of your skin rose petal soft. I glimpse a seam, powdery
White, running down your torso; you cover it with your
    arm,
As if a garment hastily stashed at the bottom
Of a drawer that I'd otherwise pay no attention.

My desire instead burns upon the finery of your
Delicate neck; I nuzzle and wait patiently until
Your hands reach for the sheets. Slowly my mouth slips to
    that chaste
Seal, grazing it, caressing it, as if it were your lips,
As if it were the curve of your ear, as if it were the
Soft underside of your chin. You moan, your body billows,
As if a hem brushed up by a strong wind; you allow
Me to linger upon that scar. I moan, too, satisfied
Not in my pleasure, not even for causing yours, but for
Having unfastened one hook of the shame strangling you.

Bread

Our love rose like bread.
Pulled from the same prairie soils,
I am the grain, the salt, the butter,
You the yeast and sugar and water,
Stirred then kneaded in courtship
Born in the heated charcoals of our
Passions, warmed to perfection,
Left upon the window to mature,
As sun crosses an azure sky
Toward inevitable twilight.

The aroma given
Off by our gazes upon one
Another draws the attention of
The hungry and full alike. Bread is
Hope they can hold in their small hands;
Others need us, for without they lack
The nourishment of dreams. We are
The daily bread of forlorn lovers,
Of all who want to believe in
Love; they cannot live without a taste.

As if Burning Aloft

As if fire feeding life, five petals shine
Like a star, brighter on the soft edges,
Center darker to draw curious eyes'
Attention, two purple-blushed flares dance
On each violet blade, radiating bright,
Exploding from the pistil, within which
Lays golden seeds, jewels resting on silk,
Patiently waiting to burst up and spread
Burning specks, potent grains of energy,
Out toward the universe, where they'll
Float until finding a spot of their own
To enliven space with majestic peace.

Questions for Lovers

How does a heart
Beat louder than thunder?

If my dream comes true,
Is truth then only a dream?

If a flower grew wings,
Would it take flight like a butterfly?

If I were on the moon,
Would you step across the stars to reach me?

Moon

Two lovers contemplating the moon we are.
My love, I sense the torment behind your eyes,
The dark water that you are forced to wade,
Then you rest your cold temple against my chest
As if reverently seeking salvation.

But my thoughts fail me now, my love, I feel you
Slipping from me like a wet fish in my hands.
I cannot trap what troubles you, can't fathom
Those shadows of darkness growing in your mind,
So my palm presses your frame tighter to mine.

Our iridescent moon swims through the long night.
Nets of stars cannot entangle it. The black sea
Gleams as I grasp for that orb to pull it down.
Your raven hair glitters blue and coral; I
Sigh once more, for I want to drown in your glow.

You look up for a moment; I cup your chin.
Calm fills your eyes, a placid lake glittering
With lucidity. At last, you've returned.
We hold on tight, afraid if we let go, this
Moment will fade like a dream into nothingness.

Shadow

Your shadow hovers over you like a puppet master
Pulling the strings of your moods and thoughts 'til I no
    longer
Know who you are. We all drag along a shadow, a stain
That follows us eternally down each dim road we walk,
But yours scales your back, leaving you hunched under its
    weight,
As it seeks a cracked window to sneak into your mind.

Hearing the crash of someone breaking in, your soul draws
    back,
Then trips into some black abyss, futilely clambers
The walls while that phantom thief dances to the flames
    burning
Your thoughts. Why should it hide? This creeping shadow
    hardly is
A match; it's sickly, ashen in hue, distorted in all
Detail, hardly strong enough to lift and move your slight
    frame.

You become a facsimile of yourself, cold and gray,
Until you are but a silhouette. Suddenly you rise,
Bursting like nova, only to fall back in on yourself,
As if a black hole. "They're all looking at me odd," you say;
Your reasoning turns random, disorganized, as if leaves
Let loose in a great whirlwind while the sky darkens to
    night.

But this shadow hides as well, intent on controlling you
From secret chambers, impervious to reason's advance.

A nighttime candle illuminates your face in amber,
You turn away. Did I catch some glint in your pupil that
Says your soul longs to be free? That it will fight? My heart
    bounds:
Climb soul, climb – even a shadow can't stay invisible!

Asleep

"There is nothing more dangerous than a man with dreams,"
    they say.
So each night as fairy clouds roll across a luminous moon,
When gold stars pulsate amid swirling darkness while we
    lay there,
Two lovers lost in our faith, I wrap an arm about your waist,
Hoping that by pulling you next to my warm heart, our
    harmonious
Rhythm will soothe away your past's demons that now
    bring nightmares.
Sometimes at night as the moon's halo wanes, you grip my
    hand, and
I dare wonder if you dream of it never leaving your side.
You lay blissfully asleep, soft as a dove. No, they are wrong.
I say there is nothing more dangerous than a man with
    hope.

Nightstalker

Your shadow snuck inside you again,
I can see it skulking behind your
Pupils, hobbling on its crippled feet,
Can see its twisted reach grabbing your
Thoughts, stuffing them in its shouldered
Bag, knocking over whatever stands
In the way. This phantom disregards
My words' reasoned flashes of light
Vainly aimed at urging it out.

Your eyes gray; that damn masked shadow
Extinguished your brightness again.
Then you instantly dissolve – you still
Sit there, still speak to, still gaze at me,
But you're in another universe
Conversing with my alter ego,
Your thoughts a shattered jar I can
Never put together; then your face
Darkens like a water-soaked street.

I know the real you sits lost again
In some dark labyrinth. I want to force
That shadow out; does it think it can
Hide in there? Does that shadow fancy
It can take your soul's place? I wait. Your
Soul will break its ropes, loosen the gag,
Will reclaim its body. Until then,
We've lost another hour...then day...and
I only can wonder where you are.

Birdwings

You lay still, quiet in your own dark,
Wounded by that returning shadow:
Your pupils ashen, your face like a
Wilted white flower, your once pink lips
Drained of their color, your graceful
Body pinned beneath a blanket.

Outside, a crowned sun reigns over
Young blue skies and warm salt-tinged air,
Magnolia blossoms burst forth from
Their green nests, the tanager's song flows
Like a rippling river. Your shadow,
Though, says you will not soar there today.

I bring water to your parched mouth,
I caress your long face, brush a small
Feathering of hair from your temple.
But my fingers are not scalpels or
Sutures, they cannot mend broken wings
For you to fly again. And I weep.

Threads

You've left but not entirely. On the floor I find a button lost from a blouse, threads from your crafts, strands of your hair, reminders of a life together that unraveled.

It's like walking through ruins, impressions of where furniture legs once stood like postholes in the carpet, my belongings tipped and scattered everywhere, a sewing needle dropped long ago and lost in the forest of carpet fibers now a thorn in my bare foot.

The steady, soothing *tick, tick, tick* of your wall clock, of your rhythms, is gone.

The noontide sun of your table lamps, of your brightness, is gone.

The soft warmth of your blankets, of your reassurance, is gone.

When I held you, I held everything there was; now I hold nothing but silence. I leave the remains where they rest, lest like ashes swept away by the wind, you fade and entirely disappear.

Questions for Scorned Lovers

Does the last woman I love
Now dance to the rhythm of my broken heart?

Is nothing lonelier than
A wind-ravaged tree beneath the infinite desert sky?

Is there any deeper abyss
Than a loved one you cannot fathom?

Are the eyes of a scorned lover
Any color other than that of bruised fruit?

Falling Rain

I wish to hear falling rain; it reminds me
Of your voice, fluid and lithesome, of that first
Step you take in the morning springing upon
The floor, of your long fingers caressing my face.

My being is parched Earth when you are not
Near, my love, it withers, is void of any
Purpose and meaning. My spirit's thirst remains
Unquenchable. I long to drown in your presence.

If You Said, 'Come Seek Me'

If you said, "Come seek me, I am on a street,"
To find you, I would walk until I ran out of road.

If you said, "Come seek me, I am on a mountain,"
To find you, I would scale every peak.

If you said, "Come seek me, I am afloat on an ocean,"
To find you, I would brave each wave.

If you said, "Come seek me, I am adrift in space,"
To find you, I would sail to all the stars.

But you do not speak, you do not ask me to seek,
So I do not know whether to walk or scale
Or brave or sail, and I am one the one left lost.

What if Stars, Not Sky, Separated Us?

This empty day drags like a slow death march,
Endless miles of roads separating us.
Hold me close in your lost soul's memory,
Don't let me slip away as if a dream.

What if stars, not sky, separated us?
How worthless it would be to scale mountains
Or compare loneliness to great canyons,
When that abyss at least has a bottom.

Though thoughts of me may be buried beneath
A tombstone erected by your shadow,
Your soul must remember when we dared
Soar higher than the sky for eternity?

It must remember. That's all that keeps my
Flayed feet moving. It must remember.

Heart-Shaped Stone

Violent cruel wind slashes off Superior,
My eyes avert to that rocky shore beneath me,
Where in beige and white cobble a black heart-shaped
Stone appears, clearer than the full moon at midnight.

I scoop up this stone, run it between my fingers,
Trace its edges just as I once did your sweet face;
I graze the heart's facet, it as flawlessly smooth
As your young cheek when my lips last caressed it.

A thin film of grit rubs off onto my fingers.
Clenching the heart, I kneel, run it quickly once, twice,
Through that lake's cold water to wash away those grains;
They swirl like stars through the night. My hands emerge
    blue.

The stone heart glistens in the sunlight, just as did
Your sable hair, while the waves' silver foam rushes
Over a firm boulder. I cannot forget you
When silhouetted pines in the wind sing your name.

I am supposed to move on, they say, go find
Another, a dozen other clichés, but my
Thoughts cannot abandon you any more than I
Can tell the waves to cease crashing against the shore.

I ponder tossing my heart to the cobble, where
Every rock is a gravestone for a love that
Perished. I gaze at the broad lake; so many
Answers remain uncatchable, like churning waves.

My arm rises to hurl that stone heart back into
The gray water from where ancient glaciers dredged
And shaped it. Let it sink and find peace. Cries of
Sea gulls, circling like harpies, urge me to heave *now*.

An icy gust slices at me, demanding that
I accept what was not our fate. I shake my head;
No, I would rather die of love than let love die.
My arm falls, my hand slips the stone in a pocket.

Let me carry it, I say to the waters, for
Just a little while longer, just a little while...

The Way to Light is to Hold Hands through the Dark

The way to light is to hold hands through the dark;
Alone, we each walk this perilous journey
On a single leg, blackness pressing at us,
Unable to distinguish shadow from soul.

Take my hand. Though we will both walk blind to one
Another, the warmth of our palms will guide us.
We will move slowly until we memorize
Each other's steps, until we see light ahead.

The darkness hisses like a serpent, the air
Chills us, oblivion rears its corpse-like stench,
But when all we've ever possessed is lost, we'll
Still own the heat of one another's hands.

When we hunger for purpose, let us hunger
Together. Coming into the light, passing
From this long hour of the dead, I promise we'll
See one another ringed in brilliance.

CREDITS

"The Dance"
Certain wording in quotation marks was provided by
J.A.R.

"Dress"
The image "it's as if a thousand butterflies abruptly
have taken flight" comes from Jean-Paul Sartre's
description of an Alexander Calder mobile.

"The Way to the Light is to Hold Hands through the Dark"
The title and opening line comes from a line in Dean
Clark's novel "Exit."

ABOUT THE AUTHOR

Rob Bignell is the owner and sole editor at Inventing Reality Editing Service, which meets the editing and proofreading needs of writers both new and published. During the past five years, he's helped more than 50 novelists, poets and nonfiction authors obtain their publishing dreams. Several of his short stories in the literary and science fiction genres have been published, and he is the author of the popular and highly acclaimed nonfiction "Hikes with Tykes" book series and the literary novel "Windmill." For more than two decades, he worked as an award-winning journalist, with half of those years spent as an editor. In addition, for seven years he served as an English and journalism instructor. He holds a Master's degree in English and a Bachelor's degree in journalism and English. "Love Letters to Sophie's Mom" marks his first collection of published poetry.

WANT TO BECOME A BETTER WRITER?

Follow the author's blog, where you'll find:

Tips for making your writing stronger

Lists of great ideas for getting published

Questions about writing
and marketing answered

Product reviews

News about the book series
and author

And more!

Visit online at:
http://inventingrealityeditingservice.typepad.
com/inventing_reality_editing/

LEARN MORE ABOUT THIS VOLUME'S POEMS

Check out the "Love Letters to Sophie's Mom" website, where you'll find:

Interview with the author

Inspirations for these poems

Thoughts about modern poetry

Reviews of the book

Photos of the author

And more!

Visit online at:
http://inventingreality.4t.com/loveletters tosophiesmom.html

Printed in Great Britain
by Amazon

17063552R00031